The Pursuit of Romance

A Husband's Guide to Thinking Beyond Chocolates, Roses and Candlelight

by
Dave and Anne Frahm

HONOR
BOOKS

The Pursuit of Romance
A Husband's Guide to Thinking Beyond Chocolates, Roses and Candlelight
ISBN 1-56292-257-2
Copyright © 1996 by Dave and Anne Frahm
6873 Prince Drive
Colorado Springs, CO 80918

Published by Honor Books, Inc.
P.O. Box 55388
Tulsa, Oklahoma 74155

3rd Printing

Published in the United States of America. All rights reserved under International Copyright Law. Contents and/or cover may not be reproduced in whole or in part in any form without the express written consent of the Publisher.

The Pursuit of Romance

A Husband's Guide to Thinking Beyond
Chocolates, Roses and Candlelight

Introduction

"I need more romance in our relationship," said my wife to me one day.

"OK," I said. "I can do that."

Settling back into my thoughts I wondered to myself, "How do I do that?"

Where does a husband begin when asked to increase his romantic output? How does he know when he's done it? Sex, I knew. But romance? Weren't they one and the same? Obviously not. I knew I was in trouble.

Off to the dictionary I flew. Let's see here..."roller coaster"

..."rolling pin"..."Roman Catholicism"..."romance."

Ah hah! There it was in black and white. Now all I had to do was read up on this romance stuff and do what Mr. Webster suggested. Here we go:

"romance"...

a medieval literary form, initially old French or Provincial, dealing with the deeds of chivalry or historical or mythological events seen in the perspective of medieval court

a love affair

the quality of being romantic

Hmmm. Big help that was. Let me try under "romantic."

"romantic"...

of or pertaining to romance, a romantic novel, a romantic situation

susceptible to romance, a romantic person

not based on facts, fanciful or exaggerated, a romantic rendering of the facts

Well, from what I could tell, Mrs. Webster was probably getting about as much romance in her marriage as Mrs. Frahm. It looked to me like Mr. Webster knew as little about the subject as I did. My tour into the land of romance had so far been dead ended.

A couple of months later Anne and I attended the wedding of a friend. It was a gala event, complete with a hoard of guests, fine cuisine, a tasty cake, and rambunctious dancing. A most memorable event, indeed. But the thing that stuck with me the most was something simple and profound the pastor had said in his charge to the couple during their ceremony.

"We all want to be pursued by another," he said. "So learn to keep on pursuing each other just like God keeps on pursuing each of us."

There are times in life when things hit just right; times when answers come to life's questions from unsuspected quarters. For me, this was one of those times—a real "Thomas Edison" experience. The lights clicked on.

Pursuit. That was it! The essence of romance! The fabric from which strong relationships are woven! Without pursuit, a relationship begins to go stale. Pursuit is to marriage like carbonation is to soda pop. Without it things go flat. The zip is gone. Things are boring, empty, unexciting. Without pursuit, marriage partners become little more than mere roommates.

"Pursuit," the finally helpful Mr. Webster wrote, "is the following after in order to capture." Having pursued Anne with vigor and creativity during our courting days, had I taken for granted that she was now mine? Had I quit trying to keep on capturing her heart? Had I gotten so caught up in the details of life and living that I'd forgotten her need for my attention, my affection, my appreciation, and intimacy? Had I forgotten that a woman is not a "soft boy;" that Anne's needs were different than mine. Had I forgotten that a woman is a responder who needs an initiator? Had I learned to take her for granted?

Yes to all. Regrettably, yes.

And so, when the idea for this book was sparked in Anne's heart, I took it upon myself to join her in the process. Not just because it would be a way for me to lavish attention on her as a co-worker in this project, but because I needed it. I needed to start thinking creatively again about how to keep on pursuing my wife, how to keep on capturing her heart and showing her that she had mine. I needed it because I, like Anne, wanted more out of my marriage.

For all you men out there who are asking the question, "How can I get more out of my marriage?" look no further than putting more energy into pursuing your wife. I guarantee that you'll reap pleasant rewards.

In the following pages we present 101 ideas to get you started. Some will fit your specific style, personality, and circumstances of life. Some may not. In the end, however, use these ideas as a springboard to your own creativity as you seek to keep on capturing your wife's heart. If she's grown accustomed to your lack of pursuit, your first attempts may be met with some level of suspicion. But remember, she's a responder. Not every lighter lights with the first flick.

*"**S**omeday after we have mastered the air, the winds, the tides, and gravity, we will harness for God the energies of love. And then for the second time in the history of the world, man will have discovered fire."*

Teilhard de Chardin

Take her out for a meal,
lingering an hour afterwards just to talk.

Surprise and creativity spark the fires of romance.

Put a note in each of seven balloons,
listing on each an activity or goodie
you know she'd like.
Let her pop one balloon each day
to get her surprise.

Flowers,
like women,
bring beauty into the world.
They belong together.

Bring her flowers.

A man's body
often communicates
louder than his mouth.

When she's talking,
turn toward her.
Look her full in the face
while she speaks.

Ask about her dreams.
"If time and money were no object, what would you enjoy doing?"

*Nothing reaches deeper
into the well of a woman's heart
than the bucket that draws forth her dreams.*

Buy a helium balloon.
Write your names on it,
how many years you've been married,
and your phone number.
Then let it go.

In Biblical times,
only a servant would touch
the feet of another.
Not only will massaging her feet
communicate your
commitment to serve her,
but it's also wonderfully relaxing.

Give her a foot massage
with her favorite moisturizer.

*There's nothing more compelling
to the human heart
than unconditional love
and acceptance.*

Tape a note
to the bathroom scale that says
"Just Right."

A woman's preferences are what make her unique, what make her interesting. Your interest in what she likes will make her feel deeply loved and desired.

Ask her about her favorites:
colors, foods, movies, songs,
days of the week,
things to do on Saturdays,
flowers, animals, perfumes,
jewelry, clothes, etc.

Arrange for a carriage
or sleigh ride
together.

Go fly a kite together.

The firm foundations of a romantic relationship are built upon the delights of surprise.

Celebrate
an "un-birthday"
by bringing her
breakfast in bed.

*Catching her off guard
now and then
adds drama to a marriage
that most women crave.*

Next time
you're in an empty elevator together,
give her a big kiss on the lips
just before the door opens.

*A woman's face
is her most important body part;
that which represents her to the
world. Your sensitive touch
communicates love and respect.*

Gently take her face in your hands, tracing her features with your fingertips like an artist drawing her face.

*The world
has yet to discover
a more direct form of pampering.*

Stock the bathroom with candles,
soft music, perfumed soaps or bath oil
beads, a fresh towel, a bowl of grapes,
a tub full of warm water, and something
wonderful and refreshing to drink.
Give her two luxurious hours to herself.

*T*his exercise can spark
unique insight into her sense of purpose,
and help her see God's hand in her life.
She'll appreciate you for it.

Ask her
if she were to write a book about her life,
what would the title be?

Start a "memories" box.
Put items in it that represent
special events in your life together.

*Such treasures, kept and coddled by her husband,
makes a woman feel cherished and loved.*

Buy seven pretty greeting cards. Make a list of seven things you like about her. Each day for a week give her a new card with an item off your list written in it.

Just words on paper.
But for her, like precious jewels
hanging from a golden chain around her neck.

*F*or many men,
signing up for dance lessons
rates right up there with
getting a tooth filled.
Your willingness to take the initiative
will speak volumes.

Sign the two of you up
for dance lessons.

Have you noticed how many magazines are directed specifically toward the female population? It's because women love them!

Bring her home a copy
of her favorite magazine.

Pull her close.
Kiss her finger tips, then the palms
of her hands. Look her in the eyes
and tell her you love her.

~~~~~~

*Sometimes the best gift is the one
you carry around in your hands all day.
Touch.*

~~~~~~

Buy her a gift certificate
from her favorite hobby store.

*He who cultivates his wife's interests
reaps an interesting partner.*

*A*ccolades before audiences
are enormous care packages
for the heart.
Hers will be in your hands.

While in her presence,
praise her in front of friends.

You'll be telling her that you know and appreciate her labors.

Surprise her
by doing a chore for her
that she normally does.

While she's sitting,
massage her shoulders.

Dedicate a song
to her
on the radio.

Men wear their bodies.
Women are their bodies.

Compliment her on her appearance.

*Keeping her just a bit
"off balance"
with creative new ways
of expressing your love and affection
heighten interest and enthusiasm.*

Send her a singing telegram.

It was just a wink.
Kind of a cute little blink.
But it began to make her think.

Catch her eye in a crowd
and wink at her.

Take her for a leisurely drive
in the country.

*Going nowhere in particular, just going...
but going with her, says you like her company
and enjoy just being together.*

Read Song of Solomon together from the Bible.

A spicy bit of biblical revelation concerning the romantic love between a husband and wife

Discovery
is a key element
woven into the fabric of romance.
Exploring the world together
opens the door
for greater discovery
of each other.

Take her on an exploration of nature in her favorite park or woodlands.

'Tis the human touch in this world that counts,
The touch of your hand and mine,
Which means far more to the fainting heart
Than shelter and bread and wine;

For shelter is gone when the night is o'er,
And bread lasts only a day,
But the touch of the hand and
the sound of the voice
Sing on in the soul alway.

Spencer Michael Free, The Human Touch

Hold her hand
whenever you walk together.

Read poetry to her.

*Poetry is to the heart
what a match is to a candle.*

Who does not love true poetry,
He lacks a bosom friend
To walk with him,
And talk with him
And all his steps attend.
Who does not love true poetry—
Its rhythmic throb and swing
The treat of it,
The sweet of it,
Along the paths of Spring.

Its joyous lilting melody
In every passing breeze,
The deep of it,
The sweep of it,
Through hours of toil or ease.
Its grandeur and sublimity—
Its majesty and might—
The feel of it,
The peal of it,
Through all the lonely night.

Its tenderness and soothing touch,
Like balm on evening air,
The feelingly
And healingly
Cures all the hurts of care.
Who does not love true poetry
Of sea and sky and sod—
The height of it,
The might of it—
He has not known his God.

Henry Clay Hall, *Who Does Not Love True Poetry?*

Rent a love story type movie
to watch together.

Ideas: "Forever Young," "Always,"
"Sleepless in Seattle,"
"Much Ado About Nothing"

Bring her a glass
of white grape juice in a goblet.
Let her take a drink,
then kiss her lips to taste it.

Art
feeds and inspires
the human soul
to give of itself to others.

Take her to an art gallery.

*Two turning together toward God
form a very strong bond.
She will appreciate your humility
expressed in dependence
upon your Lord.*

Pray with her over her concerns.

Rent a limo.
Call her and tell her to be ready
by a certain time.
Arrive in the limo to pick her up,
and go for an evening drive around town.

Invite her on a long,
leisurely walk
around the neighborhood.

Write a poem about her,
presenting it as a special gift.

Wash the dishes with her,
asking about her day.

*N*o man has 'er conceived
more romantic notion than this,
Two lovers, a feast, on a quilted spread,
lost in poetic bliss.

Plan a picnic outing.
Pack a basket with some of her
favorite snacks. Take along
a blanket to spread out on.
Bring along a book of
poetry to read to her.

Turn down her side of the bed,
and leave a love note
on the pillow.

Spend several minutes
just kissing her lightly
on the face, eyelids,
forehead, nose, and chin.

You'll be saying to her,
"I'm thankful that God gave you to
me and I want everyone to know it."

Have a glamorous picture of her made and framed for your desk.

You're telling her,
"I want the world to know who you
are and that you're very important."

Have personal stationery made for her
with her name imprinted on it.

A man who esteems the opinion of his wife, finds in her a loyalty unsurpassed by all others.

Ask her opinion
on an important decision
you've got to make.

At an unsuspecting moment,
sweep her into your arms
and tell her that she's your best friend.

Always make her
your first stop
when you come home after work.

~~~~~~~~~~~~~~~~~~~~~~~~~~~~~

*She'll revel in the feeling
of being your greatest priority.*

~~~~~~~~~~~~~~~~~~~~~~~~~~~~~

If you do nothing else to build romance into your lives, do this. Have something in mind. Don't just say, "OK, so what do you want to do?"

Plan a weekly date with her.
Set aside three hours
one day each week.
Get out of the house
and do things she likes to do.

It *has long been known*
that dance stirs the passions
in the human heart.

When you hear a song,
take her in your arms and dance.

Plan an overnight getaway
at a Bed & Breakfast,
and surprise her with it.

Buy a pad of stick ups,
leaving hidden love notes
all over the house.

Put on a tape or CD
of her favorite "mood" music.

~~~~~~~~~~~~~~~~~~~~~~~~~~~~~~

Poetry ignites a flame;
music fans it.

~~~~~~~~~~~~~~~~~~~~~~~~~~~~~~

Seat her at the dinner table.

Honor bestowed
is an investment with endless returns.

A woman,
treated as "queen for a day,"
will display unending gratitude
toward her subjects.
(PS...Shave and shower.
Don't show up looking like a bum.
You are, after all,
in the service of the Queen.)

Dedicate a day to be her slave.

Take her on a short cruise.
Off-season rates are surprisingly low.

Mail her a love letter.

~~~~~~

*Try making your own envelope
out of a large magazine page
with a pretty picture
or intriguing design on it.*

~~~~~~

Get out your wedding photos
and look at them together.

Drive her to the local "lovers' lane," and neck.

If you don't have a tree in your yard, try the local woodlands.

Carve each of your initials in a tree.
Put a heart around them.

A celebration of her favorites says,
"I thoroughly enjoy your uniqueness."
There are no deeper strokes
into the heart and passion
of a woman.

For no special reason
other than you want to,
treat her to a day of her favorites:
places to go, things to do,
foods to partake of, etc....
as much as you can pack into one day.

A *heart, deeply honored,*
is the fertile ground from which
romantic love blossoms.

As a special gift,
make a snapshot collage of her life.
Include baby pictures.

*Sometimes, through silent attention,
a man ministers most profoundly
to his wife.*

When she cries or has worries,
hold her hand and listen.
No need to offer advice, unless asked.

Of all the days that fill a year, this is the one that needs your greatest attention, for this is her day. A day to celebrate her existence. Treat it with utmost care!

Put effort into planning out the details of her next birthday celebration.

Seeing evidence that God has been
taking the "lumber" of her life
and building it into a temple
to display His good works
will do wonders for her self esteem.
Her heart will bask
in this sunshine for her soul.

Design a "life resume" for her,
complete with a listing
of all her strengths, talents, and skills.
Next to each write a line or two about
how she has displayed these in the past.

Write her mom and dad thanking them for the daughter they raised. Give her a copy of the letter.

Call her during the day
just to tell her you love her
and that you've been thinking about her.

*A celebration of goals achieved
speaks to her heart that
you are deeply interested in her life.*

Buy her a special house plant
when she reaches a special goal.

Leave a love note
in her coat pocket.

Before bed,
offer to give her a scalp massage.

Bury a time capsule together
in a special location.
Put in it a love letter you want her to read
when you dig it back up.

Light a fire and snuggle up.

If you don't have a fireplace at home,
many hotel lobbies do.

Set up a table in your bedroom
for a private dinner.
Use a table cloth, your best china,
and candlelight.
Spoon feed each other.

Go to the public library. Whisper excerpts from classic romance books to each other, i.e., Romeo and Juliet.

Absence makes the heart grow fonder...especially when gifts are involved!

If you and she are to be separated
for a time by a business trip,
wrap several little gifts
to be opened, one-a-day
for each day you'll be apart.

Kidnap her for a special outing.

Sit in the back row at the movies and kiss.

A sought after wife has a satisfied heart.

When she walks alone into a crowded room, keep looking at her with a little smile on your lips that says, "She's mine."

*Gardens feed the soul
and stir the passions.*

Stroll together
through a public flower garden.

Just as the
Declaration of Independence
is celebrated with fireworks,
your Declaration of Interdependence
should send forth sparks.

Always put thought and planning
into your anniversary.

*T*wo hearts,
in common cause,
experience a bonding
hard to manufacture elsewhere.

Do volunteer work together in a soup kitchen, homeless shelter, or nursing home.

Make a large cardboard sign with an attached stake.

Write her name, followed by any form that suits you of "I love you," i.e., "You are my heart beat"... "You are my main squeeze"... "You steam my glasses..."

Stake it strategically in your yard where she'll see it next time she heads for work or to run errands.

Hire an airplane pilot
to take you on a sight-seeing tour.

Read to her in bed
from interesting books.

Open the car door for her, both getting in and getting out.

Honor and protection are powerful ambassadors to the heart of a woman.

*N*ew, unique experiences
keep a relationship from becoming
routine and boring.
A little "danger" now and then
helps to stir the caldron of romance.

Go for a hot air balloon ride together.

Get all dressed up
and take her out
to a fancy social event.

~~~~~~~~~~~~~~~~~~~~~~~~~~~~~~

Women, like diamonds,
love
the opportunity to sparkle.

~~~~~~~~~~~~~~~~~~~~~~~~~~~~~~

Go for a walk on a beach.

Leave a provocative message for her on the answering machine.

Rent a bicycle built for two
and take her for a ride...
or ride single bicycles together.

Renew your wedding vows.
Write up a new set of commitments
and pledges, then read them to her
over a meal at your favorite restaurant.

Say, "I'm sorry,"
even when you think you've been right.

*An intelligent man knows
when losing means winning.*

Buy ad space in your local newspaper.
List ten reasons why
she wins your award as wife of the year.

Take her on a shopping spree
in her favorite clothes stores.

Sometimes the best way to a lady's heart
is through the women's section.

*Creativity and imagination
are the kissing cousins of romance.*

Take her to the airport just to sit
and watch people go by.
Make up stories together
about their lives—who they are,
what they do, where they're going and why.

Give her a locket
with your picture inside.

For no reason,
other than you want to,
buy her a piece of jewelry.

"You can give without loving,
but you cannot love
without giving."

Amy Carmichael

Ask the simple question,
"What can I do for you today, honey?"

Tuck her in for a nap
when she's tired or stressed out.
Protect her from interruptions
or the tyranny of the urgent.